You, Me and the Birds

Alan Kellermann was born in Wisconsin, USA in 1979 and lives in Swansea. In 2001, he won the Eleanor B. North and Judson Q. Owen awards from Sigma Tau Delta, the International English Honor Society. In 2011 he completed a PhD in Poetry at Swansea University, where he has led seminars in creative writing.

You, Me and the Birds

Alan Kellermann

PARTHIAN

Parthian
The Old Surgery
Napier Street
Cardigan
SA43 1ED

www.parthianbooks.com

First published in 2012
© Alan Kellermann 2012
All Rights Reserved

ISBN 978-1-908069-87-0

Editor: Kathryn Gray
Cover design by www.theundercard.co.uk
Typeset by Elaine Sharples
Printed and bound by Dinefwr Press, Llandybie, Wales

Published with the financial support of the Welsh
Books Council.

Contents

Farinelli

It's said women fainted when they heard
him sing, folded into seafoam robes

of some Venus descended deus ex machina from
the breasts of clouds. Maybe because he knew

their shape – lips clamped around
a tight O – the figure they lived, a mouth

not allowed to choose its own form,
a whirlpool, consuming whatever

penetrated the current.
He wore their clothes

in the candled stage light, formed
his throat around no man's tones.

Rosy-cheeked European geisha. A farce.
Voice tautened, he carried an aria

higher than God. Men must have hated
the way women surrendered. But they never

asked if he wanted to die rich or whole before writing
his future deep and wet on the blade of a knife.

Dancing Slowly with You

If there is only enough time in the final
minutes of the twentieth century for one last dance
I would like to be dancing it slowly with you
                         Billy Collins, 'Dancing Toward Bethlehem'

My only concern
in those last minutes
is that I couldn't
leave enough fingerprints
on you to satisfy my
curiosity, even if we
were dancing slowly,
never mind that I
haven't danced in years.

No, I think
that we should dance
with our tongues and
fingers, in some dark
corridor at the edge
of the world
where we can stumble
like gangly teenagers,
only to catch each other
in familiar valleys
until the orchestra pit
empties and the earth
sighs open,
breathing us in –
still in rhythm.

Something God Doesn't Know

inside human beings is where god learns
    Rainer Maria Rilke, 'Just as the Winged Energy of Delight'

Inside human beings
under the muscle and cartilage
is the swollen cavity
where God lives
in dark, thick as water.
She lies tumoured and coughing,
hands cupped over her ears.
God gasps for a bed and pillow
somewhere to lay a liver-spotted arm
then reaches for a cigarette
because there's nothing else to reach for.
Shivering, she coughs
a dull rasp drowned in phlegm
and gastric acids.
All that's left is hope
fingering into the black—
pale blue feathers,
the red of sunrise,
and somewhere inside human beings
slick with blood and water,
God learns what it is to be human.

Apocalypse Updated

Perhaps it's not as simple as fire
descending from a shattered sky,
licking the bones of the dead
to charcoal, the entire
earth alight – a pyre
gone awry –
and our thin souls led
off to judgement by some angelic choir.
No, it will be easier for the world to die –
brimstone might be fine for mom and dad,
but our generation likes it quick –
the image barely settled in the eye
when some oafish deity decides he's had
enough, raises the remote, and – *click*.

They Always Were a Little Strange

after Louis Jenkins

It's Joseph I feel sorry for. He had the unluck to follow the Almighty (inventor of the erogenous zone), whose omnipotence and general metamorphic ability surely allowed him to fill his role perfectly. And it's no wonder Mr and Mrs Ofnazareth had so many children – Joseph trying his damnedest to outdo the Creator left Mary constantly laid out on her back, knickers at her ankles, cigarette dangling from her – *ohohoh... down a bit – to the left now... He never had this much trouble.* To occupy herself, she listed home improvements: the floor mats needed replacing and that hole in the adobe looked vaguely like Moses. Yet here's her carpenter husband banging away at her when he should be knocking up a new set of kitchen cabinets with filigreed doors. Not to mention all the sex compelled the other sons to take over Joseph's business. There was an increasing number of broken chairs piling up kerbside all over town. Their eldest, the Creator's progeny, became a bit of a discipline problem. *It's his parents,* the townspeople said, *they always were a little strange.* For a laugh, he'd partially heal the sick – he cured Ruth, wife of Eleazar, of her leprosy, but left her with a mild to fairly annoying chest cough, and Rehoboam next door, raised from the dead for the third time, came back with an awful case of halitosis. But one day, as if he realised the only thing left to rebel against was rebellion itself, he left. The local paper reported he just walked off toward the horizon and got swallowed up in the sun. *It's his parents,* the townspeople shook their heads.

5

Trafalgar Square at Night

Then was it most apparent
there are places more comfortable than home—
three o'clock streets a mosaic
punctuated with uncertain footsteps
and smoke threads weaving themselves
between the windows of London night.
There is still no getting lost:
nowhere is a place with fountains
shut off hours ago but echoing
light rain in beads on leather coats
and bronze lions. Here,
walking becomes a new home
somewhere in the tired click of soles on wet stone.

Portrait of a Lover as a Listed Building

I'm not as Corinthian as I once was,
she says, unsculpting herself of the evening:

a hairpin, removed, looses hair in acanthus
leaves to her shoulder. *It seems I've passed*

into classical. She sighs, runs fingers over
her face, the entablature familiar, time-

deepened. The mirror she embellishes
with breasts, volutes scrolled atop

her column. *I don't have the elevation*
I used to. She fills her chest with a breath,

stately. Exhaling, grooves resettle
into her corners. *It seems*

I'm becoming rusticated, too. As she pulls down
the sash, she's windowed to the city,

a turret bursts into the needled skyline.

Companion Stars

Retrograde motion, you might say,
is what the stars insist on
reminding us about our history:
we move forward only by stumbling
through our past.

I've returned just once to that London
hotel, where, by today's one-night stand-
ards, we shared nothing at all.

We drank wine from tumblers – artistes
shunning proper vessels – smoked Dunhills
mostly naked. You framed yourself
in the window, almost too Paris
for London.

And the moon scribbled orange in puddles,
survivors of a rain we hadn't noticed.

I still have, among the bones
of a sacrificed life, your photographs. Half-
drunk, two-thirds tired. Something cosmic
about photography: for a moment,
an eye's only light.

I never told you how I wanted
you on my side of your lens
as it gathers up wayward photons
and unites them for age to yellow gently.

There are celestial bodies like us slinging
around the vast black empty.
Companion stars: furies gathered
into each other's orbits, separated only
by the force that binds them.

Giles Corey

September 19, 1692. About noon at Salem, Giles Corey was press'd to death for standing mute.

Diary of Samuel Sewall

More weight—
I said, when told
to confess
witchcraft.
And the crack
of each rib
echoed it.

Not even my
collarbone left
to snap
the board along
my stem speaks:
More   More

I am
spread flat
along the earth.
Skin and bone
pressed together
into a human
continent.

More.
A hiss.
My sole
remaining
possession
escapes –
a last, red word.

Berkeley Fudge with the Luna Trio

Luna Café, September, 2001

drummer Pete rolls in
    mid-breath
saxman Berkeley grabs
him by the

     cymbal crash

throws him into the
                deep water

above
     pianoman Tom skips
smooth pebbles
    (chord   to   chord)

     rounded
as the tones Andy pulls
    from his bass
lets drop
       explode (fat bubbles)
somewhere beneath

    the surface

where we're all arranged
    learning
        one more time

how to breathe—

Separation

In the diner, she removed her middle finger and laid it on the table in front of him. *This is how much I love you,* she said. He ordered coffee from the jaundiced waitress whose smile was a peeled banana. She popped off her remaining middle finger as well. *See how much I love you?* she asked, more insistent. He shrank into the booth a little. She shook her head, blonde hair leaping between shoulders. His eyes drooped toward his coffee. She slid out of the booth and walked away. The waitress pointed to the fingers, *Are you done with these?*

John Evans Looks for the Welsh Indians

Having explored and charted the Missurie for 1,800 miles and by my Communications with the Indians this side of the Pacific Ocean... I am able to inform you that there is no such People as the Welsh Indians.

John Evans

I suppose it's easier to say you knocked
at the door and the wrong faces resolved
under the lintel. But context by contrast
is everything. She's not ferreting tulip bulbs
away for winter. He's not slathering paint
on the windowboxes. You're desperate.
Hurried. The Chardonnay you're carrying
must be warming. The taxi's left.
And you're squinting deeper, deeper
into the parlour as if the mantel clock
knew better why you'd come.

Crafting Grandfather

The door spring groans permission and I slope
under ceiling to conjure grandfather from sawdust
and scrapwood arranged in his woodshop

as if he were still planning a shelf or spoon rack. The
bare bulb clicks alight. Resolve: Grandfather at his
table, template over graph paper, styles final lines on a
      new pattern.

Hunches over the jigsaw first-biting naked pine. Sound
rebounds from the corners of the room – the echo's
opposite: a rasp ever-louder against the ear – sawblade

whines around a curve's last few eighths of an inch.
The scream falls; the blade,
                  free again. He ranges
the Kodachromed room at the speed of imagination.

Sawdust falls from his red cardigan. He raises
a board to the bare bulb, watches the grain divide
light. A Marlboro burns itself to a stump in his lips.

He wedges sandpaper in the cleavage between
heating ducts; the Great Depression taught him to grind
off every garnet. Teaches his sons the art of the
      bandsaw:

his hands atop theirs – old leaves over new. At the
router he guides board against bit. Grandfather works
dowels on the lathe, rebirths them with grooves I trace,

old body falling to the floor in perfect curls.
Grandfather, wearing the smell of fresh sawing, drilling,
sanding settled in his sunken cheeks. Finally,
                    brushing woodchips from his hair, he bows

as if thanking the shop for accommodating him.
As my imagination fails and Grandfather fades, he
shakes my hand in sawdust, in the dry tang of cut
        wood.

(Don't Fence Me In)

When I come back someone will be singing
in an upstairs room, and I will stop
just inside the door to hear who it is,
or is it someone I don't know, singing,
in my father's house, when I come back?
                    Galway Kinnell, 'Memories of My Father'

Father, I still remember
your songs before bedtime
sung in a key all your own.
But that was what made them real –
cowboys in Stetsons, dust-dry,
leatherclad. Dirty
                    just like me
after a summer's day.
Your 'Don't Fence Me In'
was better than Autry
because you were singing
to me, not a microphone.

I believed in those wide
open spaces where the real
America began. Somewhere beyond
mountains, the earth stopped
and left some of itself behind
before stretching out into white
grass and red soil.
It was land some only touched
for a moment. I knew it
every night until I was four –
a whisper
under your thick moustache.

There are fences all across America.

Dear Lizzy,

I can't remember your face any more (I'm
sorry), can't forget the way you looked up at me,
dissolving right there, into base molecules.
But we couldn't just leave you scrabbling
around on your hands and knees as if someone
just paved over your identity. Do you remember crossing
the road? Blood heavy with chemicals, uncertain
where the earth would be next, the whole planet
trying to shake you loose. Maybe it was
                                              your name
you lost back in the road. You owled me
when I asked, as if my voice were pulsing
toward you in points of light shot through stained glass.
You looked drowned inside; gone somewhere so deep
no amount of calling would bring you back
                                              to your surface.
The police couldn't reach you either. You just sank
deeper, looking frail
                      framed by the crisp uniforms of women
who I was sure were not born, but forged
from old shields. Do you remember struggling –
fingers wormed around your reedy wrists? Your head
pushed so hard against the glass I thought you might
    shatter
scatter
        what little there was left of you across
the pavement. Even as the ambulance came, blue
and screaming, we swept you into a corner,
a broken bottle fractured along the asphalt.

Shaking Off Old Rain

One cemetery morning, the new year in its infancy,
you, who might have been my first love, come back
    to me in this lake's Monet reflections.

I turn my collar against wind that slaps my cheek
like the flat side of a knife, bless you with wings
    and free you once again

over this waterbowl carved from spongy earth, over
the asphalt knotwork laid out in black
    cords reining the trees in,

far above me where the world breathes and
birds describe spirals in orbit of lost planets.
    You always return transformed –

a slice of orange coat in the eyelet between pines,
the neon grass, drunk on the wet season.
    But you won't know this

morning's moist kiss that shades stone and concrete.
Instead, you've become an occasion – rain's abbreviated
    eruption, spreading across my skin in concentric waves.

Chandrasekhar Limit

There is something smooth
about the night
wounded
by the moon
cutting a white swath
through the black.
Sometimes dust congregates
out there, scattering
a star's light like billiard balls.
That light has had millions of years
of travel time –
a long stretch between planets –
before settling in the eye,
cool and faint.
Maybe that's why people
love the night:
everyone wants that fusion –
wants to go supernova.

The New Order

After the scandal, everybody resigned.
Work became a game
of musical chairs. I woke early
one morning and became High
Commissioner for Commemorative Plates.
Quality suffered, but nobody cracked.
The next, I got the lead in a panto.
Snow White. The new order
wasn't gender-sensitive. We met
the thirty-third day, team-teaching
a microwave cookery course
for singles. Half the chairs were empty.
So we examined spreading activation
until the sun was a penny slotted between river-
banks. *Who are we when the music stops?*
You shadowed the moment. A pigeon
in a Woolworth's sign, I perched
on an answer I couldn't voice, filling
the O where the emptiness is.

Letter from a Son in Swansea

I'll send a letter with sea-sand and salt
    dried on my right hand
once bathed in Swansea Bay. And
you, too, can touch what I stand

in at night on tentative feet. Here, I'm
    far from our greying concrete
town and cement-shouldered street.
Out here, I hear a heartbeat –

a steady sound – wasted, sad and singing
    to the half-moon and me.
Makes me wish I might truly
send – not sand, but sounds of sea.

like wallpaper she was

air-plain jetting through
my thoughts i think
i'll have another
beer in mind
she was so plain
as the nose on her
face it you wouldn't
have a chance with her
skin was pale as pearls of
wisdom teeth tight and normal-
ly i wouldn't think i'd
notice her like wallpaper she
was so unremarkable i
couldn't take my eyes
off we go into the wild
blue jeans and a white button-
up go my eyes along her
length stopping at her
head on my pint
clinging to the side-
long glances i'm giving her
trying to catch her
eye don't believe
in love at first
sight of her featureless
features simple as
the palm of her h-
and-y warhol pragmatic
the way she was painted to-

get-her i'd need to be
simple as a wrench-
ed away my
eyes wanting to read her skin
like the grain in
wood love to have her
define the rooms
i live in like wallpaper
she was

Somehow, there were no leaves

Somehow, there were no leaves
in front of the neighbours' & it was quiet
too. The gate latched if they
weren't passing through it. Drapes
opened for appropriate daytime hours.

Nobody in the window, as if they
lived in corners like umbrella-
stands.
      It could have been any Sunday
morning. I had learned long ago to tune out
my housemates fighting overhead. Today,
without a conciliatory fuck.
               & this Sunday
I noticed voices on another side
of my wall. Discussion, not argument.
Then hoovering. Some singing. Voices
again: thin, poured like whisky.

Outside it was still quiet. & somehow
there were no leaves next door, though
our house was holding summer's funeral.

Still Life with Wine Glasses

for Ashley

We hung at the bar, twisting, a little
too hard, the stems of our wine glasses.

Eight years it's been and even cancer
couldn't have you. So I'd never

have been strong enough. Still haven't
scrubbed out the scuff marks you circled

with your heel; ground out a full-
stop to a short sentence. On this new year's

doorstep, you gift me snapshots
from a life I'll never see again: lofted beds

on rickety splints, a barroom reeking
of piss, a dodgy condom.

So much has changed, you say. We've begun
filling the space between us with clichés. We wear

adulthood like battle decorations: I've sheared
off to a new continent. My accent is different now.

And you, who always wanted her mother's apron,
feel good, as you imagined, with each tug

on those strings. It's enough. An hour faded
from the new year, your embrace, warm,

reserved for an old friend. *You still
smell the same* – a whisper,

and two empty glasses.

Cain

Remember, brother, this once-pasture where you
  swallowed
my knife's flint edge? Red, like lips, encircled
the wound as if you'd asked for it.

Bone
        hewn from same bone, enseamed in skin
borrowed from the first of the line –
where I ended, you began.

From rough furrow, crack-scratched dirt, almost-
dust, I pleaded green blades up
through spit and sweat,

mixed life from ash. Above, a raven
scarred runes along the arms
of a dead oak. One dark eye

compressing everything, the other returning
only shadows. You stopped to rest
and the raven – a slash of chipped

obsidian – carved out the sun. I approached,
he threw back fire, blistered
your memory across my forehead.

It wasn't the daggers in my back
when I stood, my shoulders
peeled-beet raw, or even you,

brother, who I knew as if I'd whittled your ribs
myself. It was for my hands – cheap
tools – that I wept in young leaves.

Operation Cornflakes

I.
Some mornings, I am in the pillbox
with you. Blowing cold hands warm, only
to rest them on colder guns. *Liebe Mutter*,
you wrote. Not *Mutti* – as if you'd burned
your childhood for warmth. *They've
made me an officer*.

For that letter, I waited
three months. I'd begun to notice
how every leaf underfoot rasps
against my ribs; how heavy it is
to carry my shoulders. It used to be
the post proved I was alive. Now,
each letter through the door
could make you a memory.

                     An envelope
parachutes into the hall.
                *There's no need
to worry, Mother*. So you say. Like mail, though,
es kommt und geht. Es kommt
und geht.

II.
Never dropped mail before. He shrugs
        his shoulders, *We have our orders*.

Twenty-four and his jaw's set
as if he were going on forty. Eyes,
grey, suggest they might once have been
blue.

*In here, a minute can be anything. Had
a minute once*
                lasted a week, I swear.
                  He squints
into the bomb sight: *Everything's
a target*.
        Over the snarling Pratt & Whitneys,
the bay doors yawn open; wait to scream.
Safety released, button pressed:
                      Letters
whisper from their envelopes.

III.
For my brother's eighteenth: a rifle
and extra clips, a parachute on his back.
They dropped him into France. My two

languages buried me in England
under a sheaf of papers. I tell the enemy war
stories: how my brother is bullet-

proof. He's become a whole tank battalion,
grinding through the Ardennes.
                              I am collapsing
an empire, they tell me: the worm in an apple.

From my desk I've shelled
the Rhineland with leaflets; over breakfast,
bombed Linz with letters. It's getting harder

to imagine my brother: crunching through
snow, clutching his rifle, the secret of life.
He hasn't written in months. His last letter

said he was fine, *but the fighting's heavy and the weather's
heavier.* My sidearm on the night table isn't loaded.
I eat three meals from porcelain. All my mail arrives

home on time.

Running with a Ball

for Tommy Bowe

> *Ambition is critical.*
> David Hughes

First
      you must catch it – one
hand is sometimes enough –
two,
      three, if from an aware
teammate, or an opponent's
sausage-fingered clamp
toward your claim.

But
      hammer on, as if
through battle: shoulder
fusillades, an artillery
of elbows. Every shot
intends to bring you
down
      liberate your
prize. In short, keep it
tighter
      than a cliché.

Then
        what begins as a slice
of freedom
        off your
right shoulder, celebrates
the physics of turning
on the heel.

You've
        split wide space,
left everyone
clawing
        too late
                over
white lines as you thud
down on open green.

Stirred: The Martini Poems

Martini #1

Like sex
  with a Rhodes Scholar
she's brilliant
as light   shattered
by a gin prism
             perched
  atop the cocktail glass's
wisp of a stem

flaunts her Frank
  Lloyd Wright lines
olive eyes

reading

between the hollow
stanzas

I've composed
  in damp rings
on cocktail napkins

Martini #2

You've skewered me right
  through my pimento
and drowned me
  beneath silver ripples.
I'm just smiling like the
  bottom of a glass
emptying, washing
  away the olive brine
I've bled on your
  cherry lips.

Martini #3

Your fingers
  I noticed
were delicate as leaves

as you strained gin
  into my glass

offered it to me on
  lithe branches
I
  wanted to follow
(down)

  along your
slender trunk

to discover
in the pit
  of you

how you're able
  to leave me
  pimentoless

sinking
  into sapphire gin

Perfect Martini

You laughed   equal parts sweet and dry
across the liquid   quivering in my glass
and I knew how ice feels
                                    cracked
through its core   by gin's clean rush.

You pointed out your over-
bite   and I couldn't help but be
                                        stirred
from my depths   where you gutted me
dragged me up to my dizzy surface
and left me   a lemon twist
                                    adrift
on a cloudy sea.

Dirty Martini

I'm compressed
  into a pimento
  cupped inside her
  olive.

Her sweat like brine meets
  my gin-heavy breaths
and she sips the liquid
  moments slowly

until she empties me
  to find all that's left
  is us – olive and pimento –
slick with salt drops of each other.

Dry Martini

You're sleek
                 as a cocktail glass
I'd say
       because
                 my gaze
careering upwards
                 from your feet
needs those two Es
                 (long vowel)
to climb all the way
up
   your stem
                 to the lip
where you open
in that consonant
                 crisp
as gin
       and I plunge in
headlong –
a skewered olive
                 drowning
under subtle swells.

The Goble Poems:

Poet Crossing

Three masts crucified against an ailing moon
mark our passage through waves
for ages unsplit by curragh or coracle.

Marked men, you and I. We throw talismans
to the sea, wards, trinkets to sate
not what ranges the depths, but what mumbles

under our own currents: every traveller's fear
his discovery is not what he seeks. You
resettle your hat and lead on, parse

the sky with unsurety, a hierophant
reading scattered bones. A gannet
on the prow skitters forward, signals

the end. The island hunchbacked
under a great hall, its three doors impossible
enough to keep even memory out. An island

that marks time so we don't have to; remembers
the faces we'll not forget, but gently
surrender. You know well it's a matter of time

before we prowl through that southern door,
become strangers to the sand under our feet; even
the grass we leave behind us a sharper green.

Sleeping Woman

They are one – the knowledge and the dream.
Ambrose Bierce, *The Devil's Dictionary*

I was sailing my sofa – asleep – some
Monday in June
        the best month
for cushioned seamanship
            when I woke
to a woman aweather
          and somewhat worryingly
saw
   owling her with a look toothed
like cracked glass
         this heron-necked harbinger
glowering down, wings swept aloft
              lifted
lorded terminally over her. The look of a carrion-
crow, wilful.

How unaware she was of her still
black stalker – uncut, life-
less, but hardly deceased, a hand
               against
her cheek – a ward it seemed, or promise. I
tried to close but couldn't
           davenport navigation

being tougher than it seems.
                              My manoeuvring
was hasty in chase,
                    my ship
equipped purely for a nap. Hers, rigged
for a longer rest outran
                          with little difficulty,
my craft
        adrift, lost as last night's fantasy.

At last, lost in sunset
                        she rose
up tomorrow's side of earth, split night
open on a fresh frost – grass
stiff as talons
                shearing through
from some deeper world.

Between You Me and the Birds

One-eye-cocked you slept, as if a wink warded
off destruction. Spoke of hiding in foxholes, while
strange metals unhilled the earth around you. I never
  stopped
to consider what explosion meant until it occurred to
  me
you stood in the midst of them.

Waiting was hard, too. I drifted through rooms, turned
on lights only to shut them off. Church bells tolled and
  I forgot
to breathe. I cradled a beetroot – once – as if it were
  your heart.

Now is when I admit we were doomed. I won't. I
  stumbled
into you like a trip-wire. *Explosion*. And you inside me.

When you came back, I asked your weakness;
how to make you stay. The first cut was hardest:
  scissor-
glint screamed through candle-gasp. Each night one
  more
lock, another tuft. At your beard, I stopped: you'd
  been watching

every snip – that empty eye – as if I wasn't your
  enemy;
was the reason you'd had enough of fighting. What you
  saw
as a betrayal I meant as release: I died, too, when you
  collapsed
around me, salty pillars, the temple's ruins.

Between You Me and the Birds

I dreamt of killing your father.
Long before I ruined his house.
Began with fruits,
grapes mostly, some vines you coaxed
up stale walls.
                    Gone. There was nothing
you created I couldn't destroy.
I reduced your favourite chair
to split twigs, cracked a cat's neck
for sleeping at your feet. I nearly tore
up the stones you walked for bearing
your weight.

The bed we abused together.

As you slept, I felt guilty
watching you flicker, breathing like weak
flame; a frailty almost impossible
not to shatter. Every night, more foreign
than the last. A new confusion: arms
that stroked without swinging swords,
hands not in clutched fists.

Yours, the more sinister murder: a first lock
unnoticed. Week's end, only my beard
remained, and barely the strength
to wrap your throat in my fingers. The closer
I pulled you, the weaker my arms, thinner
my hair. I didn't know how to destroy
someone who wasn't my enemy. With two
hot-iron kisses you seared dark my world.

I scratched around your days'
edges, an unwinged crow. You, once
again your father's daughter, as if I'd only
chipped your history. Sand
and feathers you could brush away.
Forgetting was the only gift
you ever gave me; the first crack
in the lintel over our bedroom curtain.

The Chagall Poems:

Adam's Elegy

Everything's just as it was: god's eyes
polished-apple red
in the sunrise violet
on the last day.

I was cracked
from your bone and stood
beside you, a separated
                                    rib, jagged
and hemmed in your flesh.

You took what was never mine;
your fingers, fire
inside
        my thighs, burning
the dry grasses,
heat white as love.

By little deaths I consumed you
as you held my breasts, cupped
their fruit.

I swallowed
first an arm – blue
in the moistening daybreak –
then a leg
            snake peeling open
the dark and nesting in my belly.

I devoured your mane
of flame, burned white
and burst into ashy eggs.

Au Dessus de la Ville

And it's hard being dead and straining
to make up for it until you can begin to feel
a trace of eternity.
            Rainer Maria Rilke, *Duino Elegies*: The First Elegy

At night I dream fences like soldiers, shoulder-
stacked and marching out from the city where you live in

pieces – sips of coffee, teaspoon moments in monuments
erected to ourselves that we rattle around, discarded

tins marking the passing days. Are you really
any more beautiful in red brick and slate tile, leaning

on the breakfast table the way you do, knowing
morning best from every window's darker side?

I prefer you in nothing
                            more than broken
promises and red hair – enrhythmed in sleep

it seems I can climb your ribs
to the forgotten loft of you, familiar as fingertip

to latch – *click* – I unlock you
grow around you in wings stirring tornadoes

from loose soil, as we rise in knife-breaths stabbing sky-
ward – jagged armies beneath ranging across the plains.

Homage to Apollinaire

There are, of course,
                  your breasts
in relation to your whiter parts and the sheets
with the banks and pits of clouds gathered
for morning's red squint on
                              the clock
stopped
              at nineohone – time swells its cheeks
swallows us whole (inside)
we are satellites mapping
new shapes, becoming
patterns electric, occurring
and recurring along the ellipses
of spine and neck
                  your neck
arcs, creases the pillow in yellow
shadows we draw over our knotted
limbs – defence against day's
invasion peeling away
dark leaves
              an apple (green)
held
      in harmony where our bodies
unite.

Birthday

Dear Petel
    I've filled pages with just those
two words because there's nothing else
to tell you, my tongue blank as these

yellowed sheets. It is, Petel, a dialect
of silence I'm fluent in, learned
to speak as though everyone is listening, yet
nothing depends on what I've said. Why

must I cower behind a bookcase, lie
awake to the sound of words
chewed pale as skin? I'm older
today than I was yesterday, Petel,

but so many decades
can be ground into a year, how little new
it brings: two belts slung over a chair, peonies
dying from the cut, a gold bracelet

starved sunless. Today –
suddenly – I'm expected to be a woman
I wasn't yesterday, when all I want is to write
your name a thousand times, mine a thousand

more – the quietest spell, enough
to annex you to dream where
the only commodity is secrets, rooms
I've locked forgotten until you burst through

all the doors, leaping free remembered and I
hear again
        real words, phrases we needed
two mouths to speak.

The Blue House

From the sagging heart of this old man's
house the sound of a teacup
shattering traverses the river in porcelain
notes. Scratches past the man in the café
who drops a silver coin in his espresso.

Opposite, a mother weeps
at what a strange thing it is
to select tomatoes while the churchbell
chimes.
       In a flat across town, plaster
aches and cracks like eggshells
around a bricklayer in the evening
of fatherhood – a man who subdivided
this town in hardened clay and mortar
now sits sonless, hands cupping the television's
watery light.
       There is nothing fuller
or more empty than a window, thinks
the novice climbing the abbey
spire. She rests her head on the sill, looses
her blonde hair. A wayward strand
cleaves away, returning
for the teacup's clatter, the white
staccato of cracked
            bones aching,

the old man strains for a porcelain
shard; in his raisin-flesh
fingertips watches it turn green
olive, brown, then settle on his
sternum, blood-blue and cold.

The Soldier Drinks

It's one of those evenings
come screaming yellow
across the bar, the kind
when daylight refuses
to die.
      Here, only
the soldier and his cup –
and the mad evening
sky. He takes his drink
like a bullet, as if de
rigeur or decorum, then
a shot from one rifle-barrel
finger orders another.
                Light
hangs on in vermilion now,
looks foreign on the back
of his hand, and the way his hat
sits leaves dire thoughts
a hole to plug. Maybe
it's his wife again, splayed
finally,
      as she'd
threatened each time
he shipped,
        accepted
this gun, a stranger

at attention
          clasped
in her lips—
              an empty shell
falls to the bar
                crimson, the last
red of evening split wide.

The Grey House

Cattle skulls hang, threatening rain, over my return
to the city of my sins – the city I belong to but will
never inhabit. My children raised it from
mud and dry straw in porticos and parapets –
a dome boasting to dead sky.

                                I still remember
the first brick – the cornerstone in thirty years
of walls. That's the way it is with brick: one
upon another until you can't see the living
for the dead; a border you don't realise
until it's finished.

                        And always, the falcon –
hung-head and talons scritching like untended
toenails – hooking the dull cut of his mad
basalt eyes over our shoulders while we raise
his people's walls in stout brick. Houses
rising over our own built from memories
and reminiscences we stack together like sticks,
singing
        we shall rise again
                      to drown out
the rumble of history collapsing around us, tribes
divided by walls we've made – not at the end
of the lash, but from fear, only, of what leaving
means.

I still keep a tunic by the door. Its perfect
white linen reminds me of water – I was pulled
from water they say – the spray at the crest
tears loose, arcs clean and falls. Here
there's only sand swallowing the bodies
we don't have time to bury. The dead
root us an inch deeper every year, and mothers
thread their resilience into baskets for fresh reeds.

Self-Portrait with Muse

after Nigel Jenkins

At first, *cariad*, I saw you
in the magician's parlour, dusting
wings feathered equal parts smoke
and mirrors. Behind you, afternoon

blue, on which (after its sorcery stripped
us to our nakedest particles) we drew
the curtains. You showed me rare
geometries, *awen*: lines

curved furious, your fingers spidered
down to my brush. To the stroke
and circle and a pallid accent pulled
overlimb through a shadow

ambush, descending one on another
as if night meeting water. Then
having stolen (by sleight
of hand alone) the gods' fire,

we rested. Only moments,
these. Such was it always: adrift
amid myriad fleeting
mirages – some sliver

of thigh, a feather loose
upon the strand. Sometimes I forgot
what magic was, mired
in the purgatory between day-

dream and spark until, for all your mosaic
pieces, you rose from the electric
core of my atoms – a struggle
of wings against the stirring fog.

Time is a River Without Banks

No such thing, you insisted, *as flying
fish*. We were riverside on the Tawe. Remember?

The night you decided we were in love. *No reason
there can't be flying fish*, I was sure. Swansea

yawned at our feet, winking windows
at us on the riverbank. We fitted

ourselves together like terraced houses. *Fish
don't need to fly*, you asserted. Night's blue teased you

with shadows, drew borders around skin
I knew only by touch. *Time flies,* I thought

no more believable. You curled
into me, echoed the bay curving skinsmooth

to the Mumbles. *Fish don't have wings*. Smiling
head to foot, you lay bare the truth: we wore

only ourselves. *Fins*, I said, *silver – but stealing
sparks like sudden-lit candlewicks*. The city,

spooning the sea, closed her eyes,
streetlamps on fire. You were a violin

reclined on the bank. *Fins* – you meant to end it – *Fins
aren't wings, and time is wider than all the world's*

rivers, kissed end to end. I laid my bow across
and drew out hollow tones; hoped I was wrong.

Cubist Landscape

My mornings are notes
on someone else's table.
My evenings, bad
                    poker
hands shuffled in amongst
them. Afternoons are
a grocery list I keep adding
to, and when I return from
the shops in the rain –
I have only pieces. Not enough
of what I need, less than
I want. I dry them; scatter
them on the pile atop scrambled
memos to myself: 'You know,
by the end, Rita Hayworth
couldn't keep it in order,
either.' It's hard, even, to find
a piece of today without it
being interrupted: when we
met in Brynmill earlier, you
looked as young as when
I learned how a tree remembers.
Nights are rarer notes,
ever on a scrap already busy –
a train ticket to Tenby, a receipt
for toothpaste – singing
colour through the lumped
days I recognise less, as if
someone's clipped them
further, or torn away their edges.

War

for Joshua Stingl, Bagram, Afghanistan

The mountains are white horses at night, fleeting
with nightmares. By day they salute,

shoulder-pressed in ranging lines, whisper
often, of fires older than my home.

They know the inevitability of razor wire;
how mortars bloom petals

and knives. However we reshape this earth, it's our
landscape that changes. They recognise us

by our gritted teeth, though returned in different
clothes, sharper tooled. I'm grateful

my footsteps aren't lost in the stretched
evenings, or thieved by the wind. These titans,

crumpled at the horizon's feet, forgive me;
forgive all of us. They've little choice. Crooked

themselves in amongst the cloudwork, mists reverent,
a chapan riding over their shoulders and down. Look

how they rise for my camera: veterans,
bones creaking; memory quick as bullets.

The Poet Reclining

this Friday morning, to whoever is cooped up...
to him I come, and without speaking or looking
I arrive and open the door of his prison
                              Pablo Neruda, 'The Poet's Obligation'

Of course it wasn't a sombrero –
only at first glance – but
a coat
        bundled
beneath your head.

I was, admittedly, startled
when you knocked, instead
of ringing the bell like a landlord
or salesman.
                    I asked why
you'd come: for an eyeful
of sea, an acre or two of green; should I
deny an elder of my craft the blood-
purple revolution in the evening sky?

Rhossili, then. Through stonewalled
sheepfielded, hillrolling roadways.
From my fledgling Welsh, *araf*, I explained
as if there were need of it, means slow.

Your long nods spelled
                              perfect
in time with the tyres' backbeat
on asphalt; drifted again
out to the hills to wait
for inspiration come charging over
like Glyndŵr's cavalry.

We sat in the last grass closest
to the leap, while the sun groaned
toward the horizon. If a word
would have passed between us,
it could only have been
                              ymwelwr:
me, an outsider in a house I thought
I knew. You, comfortably foreign,
reclined like the gentle dead; for a pillow
your coat, the yellow of straw hats.

Paris Through the Window

for Polly Preece

I imagine it will go like this: some coffee,
and morning para-
                              chutes through
your open window. You won't need curtains.

At a café, you trace where you've
been. A few hasty scratchings on a napkin
multiplying miles by the number of days
you've been away, add the number of steps

from your door to a favourite restaurant.
It must be the exact number of windows
you can see from your flat. Since you arrived,
you've been counting them. A gift

from your father: always giving in to curiosity.
When you return, the neighbours' cat
on the window ledge reminds you of an old
love – at best, a yellow flame. You smile, only

remembering weak hands, clumsy fingers. Evening
nibbles away the roof peaks. Lights blink on;
each room aware of itself. How fortunate
then, there's still wine in the bottle

you reach for. With a glass, you watch cars reflected
in the river, because your mother taught you
people are funnier when they're upside-
down. At daylight's last wink through

the steel hatchwork lancing cloudward, you
let drops of wine stain your fingertips,
press them on the window frame. Proof
how far you've come.

The Lovers

after 'Waiting', by Yevgeny Yevtushenko

I won't wait for you
                    by the window. When
you come, I'll know it as the latch on memory's
door clicks, hear your bare heels on the stair-
case, poured into my spaces with the night, with
the rain, all wet hair and leaves left in footprints
up to my chair. There we are love letters folded
into the envelopes of each other; the night
table reddens, envious, dark unshapes us, thickening
evening until there's no room even for shadows,
and your dress, unnecessary, pools blue
at our feet.

Notes

John Evans Looks for the Welsh Indians
The quote is from *Madoc: The Making of a Myth*,
Gwyn A. Williams

Chandrasekhar Limit
Named for astrophysicist Subrahmanyan
Chandrasekhar, it describes the mass a star must reach
before going supernova. Generally given as 1.4 solar
masses.

Letter from a Son in Swansea
In three englynion.

Operation Cornflakes
World War II Office of Strategic Services missions to
airdrop propaganda, addressed like legitimate mail, at
the sites of bombed German postal trains in the hope
Deutsche Reichspost would deliver it.

Poet Crossing
Tony Goble, oil on canvas

Sleeping Woman
Tony Goble, pencil on paper

Between You Me and the Birds
Tony Goble, Watercolour

Between You Me and the Birds
Tony Goble, Watercolour

Adam's Elegy
Inspired by Le Paradis: Marc Chagall, 1961 oil on
canvas

Au Dessus de la Ville
Marc Chagall, 1924, oil on canvas

Homage to Apollinaire
Marc Chagall, 1911–12, oil on canvas

Birthday
Marc Chagall, 1915, oil on canvas

The Blue House
Marc Chagall, 1917, oil on canvas

The Soldier Drinks
Marc Chagall, 1911–12, oil on canvas

The Grey House
Marc Chagall, 1917, oil on canvas

Self-Portrait with Muse
Marc Chagall, 1917–18, oil on canvas

Time is a River Without Banks
Marc Chagall, 1930–9, oil on canvas

Cubist Landscape
Marc Chagall, 1918, oil on canvas

War
Marc Chagall, 1964–6, oil on canvas

The Poet Reclining
Marc Chagall, 1915, oil on board

Paris Through the Window
Marc Chagall, 1913, oil on canvas

The Lovers
Marc Chagall, 1911–14, oil on canvas

Acknowledgements

Acknowledgement is due to the editors of the following journals and magazines, in which poems, or versions of them, have appeared: *Agenda, New Welsh Review, Poetry Ireland Review, Main Street Rag, The Rectangle, The Seventh Quarry, Planet*. Acknowledgement is also due to the editors and publishers of anthologies in which work has appeared: *Nu: Fiction and Stuff* (Tomos Owen: Parthian), *10 of the Best* (Lucy Llewellyn: Parthian), and *Another Country: Haiku Poetry from Wales* (Nigel Jenkins, Ken Jones, Lynne Rees: Gomer)

I am indebted to Nigel Jenkins, Laurie MacDiarmid, and Richard Jones for their scrutiny and unabashed honesty, and to my editor Kathryn Gray for her brilliant work, despite my – often woeful – inefficiency.

Finally, I am grateful to Jo Furber for being, in turns, both unconditional support and unflinching critic.